D1504020

SALAD
DAYS

LIONEL MARTINEZ

Distributed by Book Club of America
150 Motor Parkway
Hauppague, NY 11788
Tel: 516-434-1932
Fax: 516-434-4865

Copyright © 1993 by Judi Olstein
Photographs © 1993 by George G. Wieser

All rights reserved.
No part of this book may be reproduced or transmitted in any form or
by any means, electronic or mechanical, including photocopying,
recording, or by any information storage and retrieval system, without
permission in writing from the Publisher.

Produced by The Triangle Group, Ltd.
227 Park Avenue
Hoboken, NJ 07030

Design: Tony Meisel
Food styling and art direction: Brock Houghten
Special thanks to Broadway Panhandler and Margot Hughes
Origination and printing: Paramount Printing Group Ltd.

Printed in Hong Kong

ISBN 0-914373-25-0

CONTENTS

INTRODUCTION

In the beginning there was lettuce, and with a little of this and some of that, it tasted good.

According to Larousse Gastronomique modern salads are "dishes made up of herbs, plants, vegetables, eggs, meat, and fish, seasoned with oil, vinegar, salt and pepper, with or without other ingredients." But until the late eighteenth century European salads were the provender of nobility. It took the French Revolution to free the chefs from the strains of noble employment and allow them to seek a new way of making a living. Thus began the classic French restaurant, which also introduced salads to the general public.

Today salads have an international flavor. Indian, Mexican, Thai and South American cuisines are but a few that have found their way to our tables. Japanese salads are a visual bouquet with ingredients cut into fans, curly shavings, rectangles and blossoms, all beautifully arranged on a serving plate. African salads use indigenous ingredients such as plantains, yams, breadfruit and cassava as well as more familiar greens. South American and Thai salads are often adorned with spicy dressings. Chinese salads are well seasoned and contained such strange fare as dried jellyfish. In short there is a world full of salads for every palate.

Salad Days contains a full spectrum of recipes ranging from the easy to the complex. The beginner will find Salad Days full of useful information and the expert will be stimulated to invent his or her own new creations. The aim of this book is to encourage the reader to master the essentials of good salad making, and then to experiment on their own. Once a cook knows the basics there is no other course in a meal that is as error-proof as a salad.

SALAD GREENS

When should you serve the green or mixed green salad? History gives us a few hints. In the first century AD, wealthy Romans, following the lead of the Emperor Domitian, went from serving their salads at the end of their large meals, to serving them at the beginning. The exact cause for this change in sequence remains unknown. What is known is that Roman hosts believed that green salads served last induced sleep among their guests. There is some truth to this notion. Lettuce is has been traditionally used in herbal medicine as a natural tranquilizer. If their salads were anywhere near the size of the rest of the Roman entrees, it's a wonder that anyone was awake to notice.

In Renaissance Italy, banquets opened with lavish and complicated salads. The Sun King, Louis XIV of France, was also a salad king. He consumed his majestic fare before, during, and after each meal. That's the way it has gone throughout history; salads were served according to the style of the moment. Today, salads are served last as an aid to digestion of rich meals; first, when the meal is simple, but the salad is complex; alone when people want to snack and watch their waistlines at the same time.

PREPARING SALAD GREENS

Freshness is the key to making great salads. Greens wilt when they have lost most of their water content. Carefully inspect all salad greens before purchasing.

When you arrive home with your fresh salad greens, wash them immediately. Washing all your greens at once removes any pesticides and other chemicals that could cause undesirable damage to the leaves, not to mention you or your family.

To wash any leafy green, including tight headed lettuce and cabbage, carefully separate the leaves and rinse them under cold water. Look for dirt near the center and at the bottom of each leaf. Always discard any wilted or bruised leaves.

Dry salad greens thoroughly. Residual water, left on the leaves from washing, has two unpleasant effects. One, water left on salad greens will draw water from the leaves, causing them to wilt. Two, wet leaves will dilute the hardiest of dressings, giving the salad soupy texture and a weak-tasting flavor. To dry salad greens, either pat the leaves dry with a paper towel, drain them in a colander, or spin them in a salad drier.

Before storing the greens you may want to tear them (never cut) into bite-sized pieces. Wrap the greens in either a cloth or paper towel, leaf by leaf if you wish. Put the towel wrapped greens in a plastic bag and put the bag in the vegetable compartment of your refrigerator. Now you will be sure to have crisp greens ready for any salad occasion.

LETTUCES

Boston lettuce is also called butterhead or cabbage lettuce. A subtle, sweet buttery flavor distinguishes this salad green. It is an excellent component in any salad and takes dressings well. Exercise caution when washing this lettuce, its leaves are fragile.
Chicory has a pleasing bitter and sharp flavor. The center leaves have a milder flavor than the other ones. This lettuce is usually used in combination with other salad greens, rarely alone.

Endive also called Belgian endive. Those familiar with this tight-leafed lettuce say it has a delicately bitter flavor. It is the cleanest of all the lettuces and rarely requires washing.

Iceberg lettuce is also called crisphead and head lettuce. The hearts of iceberg lettuce have a mild and interesting flavor; the leaves have almost none. Iceberg lettuce is very crisp and takes the heaviest of salad dressings without wilting . . . and without any loss in iceberg taste. This is the most widely sold lettuce in America.

Lamb's Lettuce

Arugula

Lamb's lettuce is known as corn salad, mâche, field salad and lamb's tongue. This tangy tasting lettuce is found both wild and cultivated in Europe. It is a fragile plant and does not travel well so it is usually available at local markets near where it is grown or picked.

Mignonette lettuce is similar to romaine lettuce in form, with dark-green or red-tinged outer leaves and a slight cashew nut-like flavor.

Oakleaf lettuce an unusual and not too common loose-headed lettuce with a distinctive flavor.

Oak leaf lettuce

Radicchio

Radicchio is the Italian member of the endive family. It comes in two colorful varieties: *rosso*, which has pink to dark red leaves with white veins, and *castelfranco*, which has green leaves with multicolored flecks. It has a strong lettuce flavor.

Romaine lettuce, also known as cos lettuce, has been characterized as having a strong, sharp, appealingly pungent taste. A very popular lettuce, it is flavorful either by itself or in combination with other greens.

Webb's lettuce is widely cultivated in the United States. It has curly leaves and is crisper than the soft leafed Boston lettuce.

OTHER GREENS

Chinese cabbage or celery cabbage tastes like a cross between celery and cabbage. Native to China and eastern Asia, Chinese cabbage is not a cabbage at all, but a white leafed member of the mustard family. It dense and crisp plant can take the heaviest of dressings without losing any flavor.

Choy sum is also called Chinese flowering cabbage. Recognizable by its small yellow flowers, large fan shaped leaves and grooved stems, choy sum has a very mild cabbage flavor.

Pak-choi is a Chinese green now cultivated in Europe and the United States. It is easily recognized by its chalk white stalks and dark green leaves. Both the succulent stalks and soft leaves have a mild cabbage flavor.

Sorrel, a lemony and tart tasting plant, which is also known as dock and sourgrass. It is grown commercially and picked in the wild. French sorrel is mildest in acidy. When used in salads, tender young leaves are the best.

Spinach is a versatile vegetable which can be used in anything from soup to stuffing. After decades of being cooked to a slimy mush, spinach as become a respected vegetable and salad green once more. As a leafy ingredient it brings a deep rich green to the salad bowl as well as its own unique taste. Spinach will bruise easily so be careful when washing and tearing its leaves.

Watercress is noted for its delicate and pungent peppery taste. It is a member of the mustard clan and was known to the Greeks in 4000 BC. Watercress leaves are fragile and bruise easily so care should be taken when washing and storing.

Chives

Watercress

HERBS

A good working knowledge of the taste of different herbs is essential to making superior salads and any other dish you wish to cook. These ubiquitous plants, many of them are actually weeds, are the secret ingredients of some of the world's greatest chefs. Using herbs in salads is the easiest way to learn about their flavors.

Unless sprigs of fresh herbs are being used a garnish, they should be finely chopped. If fresh herbs are not available dried herbs are perfectly acceptable. Dried herbs are handled somewhat differently than fresh herbs. The rule of thumb for substitution of dried for fresh is one third to one. If a recipe calls for one tablespoon of fresh herbs then the substitution of dried is one teaspoon. (One teaspoon equals one third of a tablespoon.)

Before adding the dried herbs to your recipe you should either: add the dried herbs to 1 to 2 tablespoons of any liquid called for in the recipe and let stand for 15 minutes or crush the dried herbs between fingers until they are powdered and then add them to you recipe. The first method will release more herb flavor than the second.

Fresh herbs can be stored in a tightly-sealed jar after being washed and thoroughly dried or they can be wrapped in a damp paper towel and refrigerated until you are ready to use them. If you intend to store fresh herbs, store them whole. Any cutting or chopping should be done when you use them.

Left to right: Thyme, Tarragon, Dill, Basil and Oregano

Basil a pungent member of the mint clan. Its flavor is reminiscent of cloves with a hint of licorice. Fresh basil is bright green, but turns pale brown when dried.

Chives have a mild onion-like flavor, chives work well as both a garish and a secret dressing ingredient.

Coriander, also known as cilantro and Chinese parsley, is a popular addition in Asian and Caribbean salads.

Dill is a cousin to parsley, when fresh it has a feathery top. When chopped and dried it is called dill weed. In both cases it has a taste that is reminiscent of caraway seeds.

Marjoram another member of the house of mint, it is aromatic with (what else?) minty overtones and a sweet and spicy taste. It is a good addition to mixed green and chicken salads.

Mint this strong distinctive herb has a unique flavor which cannot be compared to anything else. Use mint, fresh or dried in yogurt dressings, vegetable salads and tabouleh.

Oregano a close relative to marjoram, it was popularized in the 40's as the "pizza herb". It has a strong aromatic taste and adds zest to most seafood salads.

Parsley is a universal herb with a very agreeable flavor. It goes well with any salad except fruit.

Sage is a strong tasting pungent, perennial herb. Use sparingly with duck, veal and pork salads.

Tarragon is a subtle and elegant French herb with a slightly anise taste. Its appeal is worldwide and works well with salads ranging from mixed greens to seafood.

Thyme has a strong sharp taste. The leaves, from a perennial plant of the mint family, makes a good aromatic addition to vegetable and tomato salads.

SPICES

Herbs are best when they are fresh, but spices, even when they are considered to be fresh, are still dried. For example, the common peppercorn is really a dried berry, cloves are the dried buds from the clove tree, cinnamon is ground from dried bark, nutmeg is a dried kernel, and turmeric comes from a dried root.

Once a spice is ground it starts losing its freshness. Over time most of the essential oils and esters evaporate, leaving a tasteless powered dust in the jar.

It is important to properly store ground spice. Make sure that bottle or jar that contains the spice has an air tight seal. Keep spices in a dry, cool, dark place. Do not keep spices near a heat source, like a stove, etc. Heat will cause the spices to quickly lose their flavor.

The easiest way to always have a supply of fresh spices is to grind them yourself. All you need is an electric coffee grinder and some whole spices. Many health-food shops sell herbs and spices in their whole form.

Some spices, like chili peppers and ginger root, are best used in their non-dried state. To keep hot chili peppers fresh, put them in a brown paper bag before you store them in the refrigerator. This will keep the oils in the chili peppers from evaporating. To store ginger root, either keep it at room temperature or, believe it or not, bury the root in moist earth or sand.

Cardamom originates from seeds obtained from a cousin to the ginger root. The ground seeds are commonly used in combination with other spices such as those found in curry powder.

Cayenne pepper is a very hot spice made from ground red chili peppers. It is an essential ingredient in most curries and should be used sparingly in cheese and fish salads.

Cinnamon is the dried ground bark of the cinnamon tree. Light yellowish-brown in color, its tangy aromatic flavor goes well with fruit salads.

Cloves are the dried buds of the evergreen clove tree. Strong in flavor, they are often used in conjunction with cinnamon in most recipes.

Cumin really belongs to the carrot family. The ground seeds are an important in most curry powders and chili con carne recipes.

Curry powder is made from a combination of spices like turmeric, clove, cayenne, cumin, mustard seed, coriander, cardamom and ginger.

Ginger is the root of a perennial plant. Best used fresh for flavoring fruit salads.

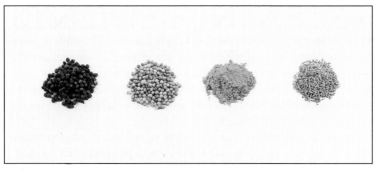

Left to right: Black Pepper, White Pepper, Curry and Cumin

Mace is the ground fibrous outer husk of the nutmeg seed. It is widely used in fruit salads, chocolate puddings and cakes to bring out a mild nutmeg flavor.

Peppercorns, both white and black, are dried berries that come from perennial vines. White peppercorns are left on the vines to ripen while black peppercorns are picked just as the ripening process has started.

Turmeric is the ground product of a dried root. It is often utilized as yellow coloring agent.

Left: Ginger, Right: Cinnamon

EXTRA INGREDIENTS

Most Americans now know that salads are more than a few pieces of iceberg lettuce, a couple of slices of tomato and an occasional cucumber. There is a whole world of salad of ingredients to choose from. Different cultures have developed many tasty basic primary foods over the centuries, and these elements are now available in most supermarkets.

All you need to open this universe of endless salad opportunities is a little imagination and a willingness to experiment. Many of the world's greatest salads combine what was once thought to be dissimilar ingredients: the French Salade Niçoise is a combination of lettuce, tuna, olives and hard boiled eggs; Greek salad adds lettuce, feta cheese, tomatoes, onions and olives together; and the Waldorf salad mixes walnuts, apples, celery, lettuce and dates in one serving bowl. These salads have one principal in common, they combine a pleasing balance of color, flavor and texture; they appeal both to the eye and the palate.

A VERY IMPORTANT EXTRA

Garlic is the king of extra ingredients. Not only is does this plant provide such health benefits, such as helping to lower high cholesterol levels in the blood and having a very mild natural antibiotic activity, it also has ability to combine dissimilar tastes found in many recipes.

For centuries cooks have used small amounts of garlic to bind flavors that ordinarily would not taste good together. This unique quality is activated anytime garlic is minced. Cutting garlic releases two natural chemicals that seek each other out in whatever liquid they happen to find themselves. When these released chemicals meet each other they coalesce to form a third chemical. This binding process drags all other extraneous flavors with it and blends them into a totally new taste.

OTHER EXTRA INGREDIENTS

Almonds, must be blanched to remove the bitter skins after they have been shelled. Use these flat, tan nuts whole, flaked or chopped in your favorite salad for a crunchy change of pace.

Bamboo shoots are noted for their crisp texture and mild, nut-like taste.

Bean sprouts are baby beans that have just germinated producing tiny, nutritious shoots.

Cannellini beans are Italian white beans similar to haricot beans. They add substance as well as flavor to a salad and take dressings well.

Capers are the flower buds of a mustard plant. They are usually sold pickled and have a sour salty taste.

Cashews are crunchy, flavorsome nuts that are usually sold shelled. Avoid using ready-salted cashews as a salad ingredient.

Left to right: Lentils, Pine Nuts, Almonds and Sesame Seeds

Chick peas are mealy, substantial pulses with a sweetly bland flavor that blends well with more assertive ingredients.

Couscous is a grain product derived from durum wheat. Its bland flavor is enlivened in salads with the addition of herbs and spices.

Lentils come in a variety of colors including red, brown, orange and green. Used whole or split, they must be cooked before adding them to salads.

Lotus root is crunchy and bland, prized in Asia for its decorative pattern when sliced.

Mung bean sprouts are frequently used in Asian and health-food salads.

Pine nuts are used extensively in the cuisines of Italy, Greece and the Middle East. They have a sweet flavor and are best used in salads after they have been lightlt roasted in a small frying pan.

Sesame Seeds are used in many cuisines, especially in Asia, They add a delicious crunch to candies, baked goods and salads.

Tofu (bean curd) is made from yellow soy beans and is sold in soft, moist cubes. It has a delicate texture and clean fragrance.

Walnuts, distinctive looking and strong-tasting, they have long been a popular addition to the American salad bowl.

Water chestnuts are a frequent addition to many Chinese dishes and salads. They are available, either fresh or in cans, at better supermarkets and Asian specialty stores.

DRESSINGS

If clothes make the person, the dressings make the salad. The purpose is the same: to flatter without distracting. In fact salads have been dressed ever since ancient times.

The very word salad implies the need to be dressed, since salad derives from the Latin word *sal*, which means salt. Salt was one of the first recorded dressings used in ancient Rome and remains a key ingredient to this day.

There are four primary bases for a salad dressing: oil, vinegar or lemon juice, salt or a salty sauce like Asian soy and mayonnaise. Combinations of these basic elements have led to an infinite variety of dressings.

OILS AND VINEGARS

About 90 percent of all salad dressings contain oil both and vinegar. Some dressings, like homemade mayonnaise, do not resemble the traditional salad vinaigrette, and yet they contain oil and vinegar. The more you know about the available oils and vinegars the better your salad dressings will be.

OLIVE OILS

The most frequently used oil in salad dressings is olive oil. To some it is the only oil of culinary importance. Although there are other oils, olive oil is the oldest oil used in cooking. Its history stretches back 5000 years ago to the cradle of civilization, ancient Mesopotamia. No other oil as remained as popular though the ages, as empires rose and fell, as the fruity oil of the olive.

Olive oil comes in five quality ratings. This system is based on the processing of the oil and not necessarily on the excellence of the olive.

Extra virgin olive oil is the product of the first cold pressing of the olive harvest and the most intensely flavored. Depending on the amount of filtering it has undergone, this oil tends to range in color between light yellowish-green to dark green. It is the best olive oil for salads.

Virgin olive oil is a deep yellow in color. This grade is a combination of oils from the last part of the first cold pressing plus the entire second cold pressing of the olives. It is a moderately flavorful oil, lighter in texture and taste than the extra virgin oils. Although it is an excellent salad oil, virgin olive oil is not widely available in America.

Pure olive oil is the most widely sold grade of olive in the United States. It is of commercial quality and retains some olive taste. Pure olive oil is a refined oil, which means it is produced from the heat and solvent treated mash left over from the first two olive pressings. Of all the olive oils that work well in salad dressings, the pure grade of oil is least expensive. Unfortunately the low price also means low flavor.

Fine Olive oil is not to be used for salads. This oil is the product of intense chemical and heat refining of the mash that was used to create pure olive oil. Often this grade of olive oil contains a blend of other vegetable oils.

Extra extra virgin olive oil is the rarest of all olive oils. It is produced from just the first few twists of the olive press. A dark green, intensely flavored oil, it is too expensive to mix in any quantity with other ingredients. The best way to use this oil on a salad is to sprinkle the lettuce leaves with this extraordinary oil, then add a little salt, followed by a few drops of balsamic vinegar.

The price of olive oil has much to do with which pressing you buy. Extra virgin olive oil is almost twice as expensive as pure olive oil. Extra extra virgin olive oil can be two to three times more costly than the extra virgin variety.

The country of origin also figures in the pricing of olive oil. French oils, with their light golden color and fruity taste, are the most expensive and are considered by francophiles to be the best in world. The Greek and Italian olive oils are less costly than the French varieties and are hardy, robust and aromatic. Due to its heaviness, Spanish olive oil is more suited to cooking than salad dressings.

Left to right: Extra Virgin, Virgin and Pure Olive Oils

OTHER OILS

Of course there are other oils that can be used for salad dressings. Many in use today also have deep roots in history. Flax and radish seed oils were first used by the ancient Egyptians. The early Asians utilized soya beans and coconuts as sources for their oil. One oil definitely not in use today was extracted from the opium poppy by the ancient Greeks. This poppy seed oil must have produced a rather dreamy, if not addictive, dressing.

Grape seed oil is a rich, full-bodied oil usually found in combination with pepper and/or herbs.

Hazelnut and almond oils are delicate, nutty tasting oils. They are very light and are used on subtlety flavored salad greens. Not cheap, these oils require refrigeration to protect their fresh flavor.

Peanut oil is extensively used in South-East Asian cooking. The peanut taste is not pronounced and it can be used in making heavily flavored dressings.

Salad oil is a mixture of those vegetable oils which, depending on world commodity prices at the time of bottling, a manufacturer can buy cheaply. The same brand many contain cottonseed oil mixed with coconut oil one month and all corn oil the next. Salad oil is a good value if all you are concerned with is price.

Sesame oil is an aromatic oil much used in Asian cooking. As the name implies the oil is extracted from crushed sesame seeds. When used in combination with blander salad oils, a few drops of sesame oil will impart a mysterious savor.

Sunflower seed, corn, cottonwood, safflower and soya bean oils are rather bland in taste and texture. Each of these oils has just a hint of their origins in their taste. The polyunsaturated oils, like soya bean, safflower and corn, are mainly used for their health benefits.

Walnut oil is a very aromatic oil that imparts an intense nutty taste to dressings. It also makes an interesting mayonnaise that goes well with chicken salad. Walnut is expensive; keep under refrigeration to maintain its freshness.

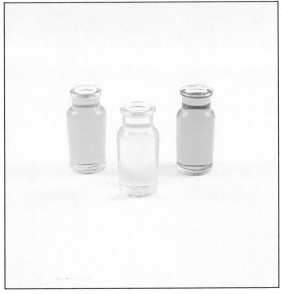

Left to right: Peanut, Salad and Walnut Oils

VINEGARS

First made by the Chinese over 3,000 years ago, vinegar is the juice of any fruit or grain that has fermented beyond alcohol and become acidic. The acidic ingredient is this process is acetic acid.

Its modern name derives from the ancient Gauls, who were introduced to wine in by the Romans in first century BC. Unfortunately transportation was a very slow process then and the wine usually spoiled by the time the Romans got around to selling it to the local populace. The Gauls called this overly ripe potion *vin aigre* or sour wine.

Vinegar is used in proportion its strength. This is determined by the particular vinegar's acetic acid content. Commonly, salad vinegar's acid ranges from 4 to 6 percent. How much vinegar you use in your dressings is a matter of taste. Proportions for vinaigrette extend from the traditional French rubric of one part vinegar to three parts oil, to Elizabeth David's recommendation of one part vinegar to six parts oil.

Balsamic vinegar is a remarkable sour/sweet product of northern Italy. Aged for at least ten years in a succession of oak, chestnut, mulberry and juniper kegs, it's taste and fragrance are incomparable. By Italian law no vinegar that has not been processed by the prescribed method can be called balsamic. Keep a bottle of this special vinegar in your cupboard for those times when you want to give your favorite dressing a lift.

Cider vinegar is produced from apple juice. It is an American tradition. Use cider vinegar sparingly, its percentage of acetic acid is very high.

Wine vinegars are made from red, white, rosé wines. In Japan they use rice wine to make their vinegar; in Spain it is sometimes sherry; France, of course, occasionally gives champagne the nod to evolve into a flavorful vinegar.

Left to right: White and Red Wine Vinegars

Malt vinegar is distilled from malt and has a tart taste. Mostly consumed in the United Kingdom, it has a high acetic acid content and should be used sparingly when making salad dressings.

Distilled vinegar is the end product of grain distillation. Due to its very high acid level, it has no place in salad-making. The best use for distilled vinegar is pickling or household cleaning chores. However, in a pinch, it can be used diluted with water.

Fruit vinegars are vinegars fermented from such fruits as pears and plums. Other fruit vinegars are really wine vinegars that have the fruit added at either the wine or vinegar stage. In either case, their light, fresh flavor makes a wonderful addition to the salad dressing spectrum. They can be made at home (see Fresh Fruit Vinegar) or bought from specialist food shops.

Herb vinegars are vinegars in which herbs such as basil, rosemary, or tarragon have been steeped. Herb vinegars can change an everyday day salad dressing into a new taste adventure. They are available commercially or can be made at home (see Herb Vinegar). Other flavorings added to vinegars include garlic, honey and lemon rind.

Left to right: Red Wine-Thyme and White Wine-Tarragon Vinegars

VINEGAR HINTS

The party is over and you find a few drops of wine left at the bottom of several bottles. Don't throw it away. Add the wine to your vinegar supply: red wine to the red vinegar and white wine to your white vinegar. The wine will naturally sour in the vinegar bottle, creating the impression of an endless supply of vinegar.

Do not serve a salad with a vinegar dressing on painted plates. At the very least the vinegar will corrode the paint; at the worst, the vinegar will leach the lead out of paint, causing a health hazard.

FRESH HERB VINEGAR

Fresh herb vinegars add a depth of flavor to salad dressings., marinades and pickles. Suggested herbs include tarragon, basil, rosemary, thyme, whole garlic cloves and coarsely chopped shallots. You may use as little or many varieties as you like.

1 1/2 cups fresh herbs, washed and blotted dry
4 cups white or red wine vinegar

Place the herbs in a large jar and add the vinegar. Stir the herb and vinegar mixture. Seal the jar and store in a dark place for 6 weeks. Shake the jar every few days.

Remove the jar from storage and strain the vinegar through into smaller, sterilized bottles. Discard the used herbs. Add a few sprigs of fresh herbs to each bottle. Tightly seal the bottles and store away from direct light. Makes 1 quart.

Fresh Herb Vinegar, Garlic Variation: Put a clove of garlic in with the vinegar and herbs for twenty four hours. Remove and discard.

FRUIT VINEGAR

Fruit flavored vinegar can be made from raspberries, blueberries, blackberries, currants, cherries and pears.

2 cups white wine vinegar
3/4 cup fresh fruit, washed, dried and coarsely chopped
3 tablespoons sugar

Place the fruit in a large jar and add the vinegar. Stir the mixture. Seal the jar and store in a dark place for 2 weeks. Shake the jar once or twice during its storage.

Strain the vinegar through into smaller sterilized bottles. Discard the used fruit . Tightly seal the bottles and store away from direct light.

1. Peel a clove of garlic by crushing it with the side of a knife blade.

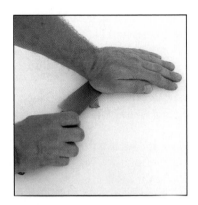

2. Slice the garlic thinly.

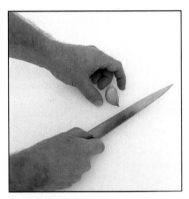

3. Chop the garlic until almost a puree.

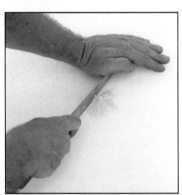

4. Add a generous teaspoon of Dijon mustard.

VINAIGRETTE

5. Grind in a few turns of black pepper.

6. Add the olive oil.

7. Add the wine vinegar; use very little, as the mustard will cut the oil.

8. Whisk all the ingredients together until well-blended.

CLASSIC FRENCH VINAIGRETTE

Centuries ago this was the quick and easy way to dress a salad without sacrificing taste. It still is. The dressing calls for oil in a ratio of three to one to the vinegar, and it calls for what to modern tastes seems to be a lot of salt. The oil to vinegar proportion should be varied to taste and the salt can easily be reduced.

2 tablespoons wine vinegar
6 tablespoons olive oil, extra virgin preferred
1 teaspoon salt
1/8 teaspoon freshly ground pepper

Put the vinegar, salt and pepper in a small wooden salad bowl. Beat the mixture with a wire whisk or fork until the salt dissolves. Add the olive oil and beat until the mixture has a creamy texture. Let stand for 5 minutes, beat once more and pour over a mixed green salad. Makes 1/2 cup.

Classic French Vinaigrette, Garlic Variation: Add 1 clove crushed garlic after the olive oil has been beaten. Let the mixture stand for 10 minutes. Remove the garlic clove and beat again.

MODERN VINAIGRETTE

Now that you have seen the classic vinaigrette, try this contemporary version. It calls for the addition of mustard, which adds a little tang to a green salad and a little lemon juice for a fresher taste. Note the modern vinaigrette requires far less salt than the classic rendition.

This recipe can easily be halved and will keep well for up to four days if covered tightly and stored in the refrigerator.

3/4 cup olive oil, extra virgin preferred
2 tablespoons wine vinegar
1 tablespoon lemon juice
1 teaspoon mustard
1/4 teaspoon salt, or to taste
1/8 teaspoon freshly ground black pepper

Put the vinegar, lemon juice, mustard, salt and pepper in a jar with a tightly fitting lid. Cover the jar tightly and shake until the salt dissolves. Add the olive oil and shake again until well mixed. Let stand for 10 minutes and shake the jar one last time. Pour over a mixed green salad. Makes 1 cup.

Garlic Variation: Add 1 clove minced garlic with the vinegar. Follow the rest of the recipe as is.

MUSTARD & THYME VINAIGRETTE

This tangy vinaigrette substitutes soya sauce for the customary salt and adds thyme for rich herbal taste. It is made in a food processor, because that is best way to blend all the ingredients. It also makes for a very smooth dressing. This is an excellent vinaigrette for a lettuce, tomato and avocado salad.

7 tablespoons olive oil
2 tablespoons red wine vinegar
1 tablespoon Dijon mustard
1/2 teaspoon dried thyme
2 teaspoons soy sauce
1 small clove garlic, coarsely chopped
1/4 teaspoon freshly ground black pepper

Put the red wine vinegar, Dijon mustard, thyme, soy sauce, garlic and black pepper into a food processor. Pulse the food processor for three seconds or until all the ingredients are well blended. Add the olive oil and pulse again until the oil has fully integrated with other ingredients. Serve. Makes 2/3 cup.

Modern Vinaigrette

Mustard-Thyme Vinaigrette

YOGURT-MUSTARD VINAIGRETTE

In this version of vinaigrette, the oil is placed by yogurt and vinegar by lemon juice. Serve it over a green salad.

1/4 cup unflavored yogurt
4 teaspoons fresh lemon juice
1 tablespoon Dijon mustard
1/2 teaspoon dried thyme
1 scallion, coarsely chopped
2 teaspoons soy sauce
1/4 teaspoon freshly ground black pepper

Put the yogurt, lemon juice, Dijon mustard, thyme, scallion, soy sauce and black pepper into a food processor. Pulse the food processor until all the ingredients are well blended. Pour over salad. Makes 1/2 cup.

LIME VINAIGRETTE

This variation of the Modern Vinaigrette goes well with seafood salads and steamed vegetables, served either hot or cold.

1/2 cup olive oil, extra virgin preferred
1/4 cup lime juice
1 clove garlic, coarsely chopped
1/4 teaspoon dill weed
1/4 teaspoon salt
2 tablespoons fresh parsley, coarsely chopped
1/4 teaspoon freshly ground black pepper

In a jar with a tight fitting lid, put the lime juice, garlic, dill weed, parsley, salt and pepper. Cover the jar tightly and shake until the salt dissolves. Add the olive oil and shake again until well mixed. Let stand for 10 minutes and shake the jar one last time. Pour over salad. Makes less than 1 cup.

MUSTARD-CREAM DRESSING

A creamy dressing that is equally at home enhancing green and vegetable salads as well being used as a crudité dip.

1 cup sour cream
2 tablespoons olive oil
2 tablespoon Dijon mustard
2 tablespoons fresh lemon juice
1 scallion, chopped
1 clove garlic, coarsely chopped
1/4 teaspoon salt

In a food processor put the sour cream, olive oil, Dijon mustard, lemon juice, scallion, garlic and salt. Process until all the ingredients are well blended. Pour over salad. Makes 1 1/2 cups.

TOUCH OF ASIA DRESSING

This dressing adds zest to a simple lettuce salad. Store in a tightly covered jar, in a refrigerator, for up to four days.

2 tablespoons soy sauce
2 teaspoons water
1 whole green onion, minced
1/2 teaspoon sesame oil
1/4 teaspoon hot pepper chile oil
1 finely chopped garlic clove
1/4 teaspoon ground black pepper
3/4 cup peanut oil
7 teaspoons rice wine vinegar

Put the soy sauce, water, green onion, sesame oil, hot pepper oil, garlic and black pepper in a jar with a tightly fitting lid. Cover and shake until all the ingredients are blended. Add the peanut oil to the jar, cover and shake again. Let the mixture stand for two minutes. Add the vinegar to the jar. Cover tightly and shake well once more. Pour over salad. Makes 1 1/2 cups.

Mustard Variation: This produces a less spicy dressing without loosing any of the tanginess. Delete the 1/4 teaspoon hot pepper oil and substitute 1/2 teaspoon Dijon mustard. Prepare as usual.

CHINESE DRESSING

Oyster sauce has a subtle but definite presence in this dressing. Use Chinese Dressing over mixed green salads and vegetable salads. It will keep well, refrigerated, in a tightly sealed container for three-five days

1 tablespoon soy sauce
1 tablespoon oyster sauce
1 garlic clove coarsely chopped
1 teaspoon fresh ginger, chopped, or 2 teaspoons dried ginger powder
6 tablespoons rice wine vinegar
3/4 cup peanut oil, any light oil may be substituted

Put the soy sauce, oyster sauce, garlic, ginger and vinegar into a food processor. Pulse the food processor for three seconds or until all the ingredients are well blended. Add the peanut oil and pulse again until the mixture has become smooth. Pour over salad
Makes 1 1/4 cups.

Chinese Dressing, Exotic Variation: Truly, Chinese five spice adds a indefinable Asian flavor to this already tasty dressing. Once a mysterious ingredient available only in Asian specialty stores, Chinese five spice is now found on supermarket shelves packaged by commercial producers of herbs and spices.
Add 1/2 teaspoon Chinese five spice along with the ginger.
Continue the recipe in the usual manner.

CORIANDER DRESSING

This dressing is at its best when left to marinate at room temperature for 20 minutes. Serve it on green and rice salads. Coriander Dressing will keep well in the refrigerator for three days.

1 1/2 tablespoons fresh coriander, or 1 1/2 teaspoons dried
1/2 teaspoon dried basil
1/2 teaspoon dried chives
1 tablespoon water
1 teaspoon Dijon mustard
1 garlic clove, finely chopped
3/4 cup light oil
3 tablespoons tarragon vinegar
1/4 teaspoon salt

Put the coriander, basil, chives, water in a jar with a tightly fitting lid. Cover the jar tightly and shake. Let stand for several minutes. Add the mustard, garlic, and shake again until well mixed. Pour the oil, vinegar, and salt into the jar. Shake the jar one last time until the salt dissolves. Pour over a mixed green salad when ready.
Makes 1 cup.

FRENCH GARDEN DRESSING

Everything in this recipe must be fresh. No dried substitutions allowed. It's wonderful with seafood, crudités, cold roast meat, poultry and of course green salads.

Both extra virgin and pure olive oil are used in this dressing. The extra virgin oil provides the intense olive flavor and pure olive oil adds body when blended in a food processor.

1/4 cup extra virgin olive oil
5 tablespoons tarragon vinegar
1 garlic clove, coarsely chopped
1/4 cup tomatoes, seeded, skinned and chopped
2 teaspoons fresh basil, chopped
1 teaspoon Dijon mustard
1 tablespoon green pepper, chopped
1 tablespoon fresh parsley, chopped
1 tablespoon onion, chopped
1/4 teaspoon salt
1/4 teaspoon freshly ground black pepper
1/2 cup pure olive oil

Put all the ingredients except the pure olive oil into a food processor. Process until all the ingredients are well blended. Add the pure olive oil and pulse again until the mixture has become smooth. Pour over salad Makes 1 1/4 cups.

PAPRIKA DRESSING

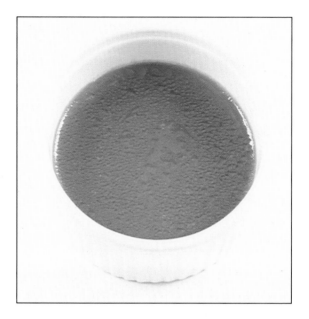

This dressing goes well with any containing mushrooms and greens. For sweeter dressing add another tablespoon of honey. This dressing will keep for three days in the refrigerator.

1 tablespoon of honey
1/2 teaspoon salt
1 1/2 tablespoons water
2 teaspoons paprika
1 tablespoon Dijon mustard
2/3 cup pure olive oil
4 tablespoons red wine vinegar
1/4 teaspoon freshly ground pepper

In a jar with tight fitting lid put the honey, salt and water. Shake until the salt and honey dissolve. Pour the honey water mixture into a food processor. Add the paprika, mustard and process for three seconds or until the ingredients are well blended. Add the olive, vinegar and pepper and pulse again until the mixture has become well mixed. Pour over salad Makes 1 1/4 cups.

Paprika-Poppy Seed Variation: It's like having two dressings with one recipe. With just a simple addition of one ingredient you can create a whole new taste and texture. Add 1 teaspoon of poppy seeds when you process the paprika and mustard.

LEMON DRESSING

This tart dressing is best when used over vegetable salads. It is also good with warm steamed vegetables. This recipe should not be halved.

1/2 cup olive oil
1/8 teaspoon salt
1 teaspoon water
1/8 teaspoons lemon rind, grated
2 teaspoons dried mint
1/4 cup fresh lemon juice
1/4 teaspoon freshly ground black pepper

Put the salt, water, lemon rind, mint and water in a jar with a tightly fitting lid. Let stand for two minutes. Add the lemon juice, olive oil and black pepper. Cover and shake. Makes 3/4 cup.

WALNUT-YOGURT DRESSING

This is a great green and chicken salad dressing. It is especially good with escarole, endive and Chinese cabbage. Walnut-yogurt dressing does not keep more than two days.

1/2 cup yogurt
3 tablespoons white wine vinegar
1 1/2 teaspoon Dijon mustard
1 clove garlic, chopped
1/2 teaspoon dried chervil
2 teaspoons walnuts, chopped
1/4 teaspoon salt
3 tablespoons walnut oil

Put the yogurt, vinegar, Dijon mustard, garlic, chervil, walnuts, and salt into a food processor. Pulse the food processor until all the ingredients are well blended. Add the walnut oil and pulse for five seconds. Pour over salad. Makes 1 cup.

Red, green and yellow peppers harmonize with many dressings.

NATIVE AMERICAN DRESSING

As a dressing, this is not a page out of history. Rather, it is a modern rendition of what the early settlers did when they made *Wilted Lettuce Salad*. Like the earlier dressing, Native American Dressing is also good on dandelion leaves and spinach.

1 cup Modern Vinaigrette
2 hard cooked egg yolks, mashed
1 clove garlic, minced
1 tablespoon parsley, finely chopped
1 tablespoon green pepper, minced
1 tablespoon sweet red pepper, minced
1 tablespoon scallion, finely chopped

Put the Modern Vinaigrette and the mashed egg yolks in a jar with tight fitting lid. Shake well. Add the remaining ingredients and shake again. Let stand for five minutes. Pour over salad. Makes 1 1/4 cups.

MY SECRET ASIAN DRESSING

Years ago I went to a now-vanished restaurant and fell in love with this marvelous salad dressing. The exact recipe was a house secret and none of waiters would tell me anything more than a fragment. After a year of prying and spying I uncovered the concealed ingredient by having one of the waiters describe the jar it came in. I rushed home and added the newly discovered element to my previously failed attempts. It worked.

Over the years the dressing evolved to its present state. I present it here for everyone to enjoy. Please note that the recipe calls for a rather exotic ingredient called *dashi*. *Dashi* is a Japanese soup base made from dried bonito fish and seaweed. It can be found in Asian specialty markets and better supermarkets.

2 teaspoons instant *dashi*
1/4 cup hot water
1 tablespoon honey
1 garlic clove, chopped
1/4 teaspoon curry powder
1 teaspoon dried tarragon
1/4 cup extra virgin olive oil
3 tablespoons tarragon vinegar
1/2 cup olive oil

Put the *dashi* and hot water in a jar and stir until the dashi completely dissolves. Pour the mixture in a food processor and add the honey, garlic, curry powder, and tarragon. Pulse for four seconds. Add the extra virgin olive oil and vinegar. Pulse once more until well blended. Add the remaining oil and pulse until the dressing has slightly thickened. Makes 1 cup.

CREAMY DRESSING

For green and tortellini salads, use this fine, all-purpose, cream-based dressing. Do not halve this recipe.

2 tablespoons wine vinegar
6 tablespoons olive oil
1/2 teaspoon salt
1/2 freshly ground black pepper
2 teaspoons Dijon-style mustard
2 garlic cloves, minced
2 teaspoons *creme fraîche* or sour cream

Put all the ingredients, except the *creme fraîche* in a jar with a tightly fitting lid. Cover and shake until the salt dissolves. Add the *creme fraîche* and shake again until well blended. Makes 1/2 cup.

Creme Fraîche: Use only fresh heavy cream in making this. Refrigerate *creme fraîche* for 12 hours before serving. It will keep, tightly covered, in the refrigerator for 5 days.

1 cup heavy cream
1-2 tablespoons buttermilk

Combine the heavy cream and buttermilk (the more buttermilk the tangier the flavor) in a jar with a tightly fitting lid. Cover the jar and shake until the ingredients are well mixed. Let the mixture stand at room temperature for 10 hours. Refrigerate until ready to use. Makes 1 cup.

HERB DRESSING

When fresh herbs are available substitute 1 1/2 teaspoons fresh for 1/2 teaspoon dried. This a good summertime green salad dressing and will keep in the refrigerator for three to five days.

1/2 teaspoon chives, dried
1/2 teaspoon chervil, dried
1/2 teaspoon summer savory, dried
1/4 teaspoon freshly ground black pepper
1/2 teaspoon salt
1 tablespoon scallion, minced
1 tablespoon fresh parsley, finely chopped
3/4 cup extra virgin olive oil
1/4 cup tarragon vinegar

Combine all the ingredients in a food processor. Pulse the food processor for six seconds or until all the ingredients are well blended. Pour over salad. Makes 1 1/4 cups.

Herb Dressing, Creamy Variation: Subtract 2 tablespoons oil and add 2 tablespoons heavy cream. Continue the recipe as usual.

ITALIAN DRESSING

For the best results do not economize on this dressing. This is an Italian Dressing, not something poured from a store bought bottle. Use extra virgin olive oil and balsamic vinegar where they are called for. Its perfect for antipasto as well as green salads. This recipe may be easily halved or doubled.

1 teaspoon basil, dried
1/4 teaspoon oregano, dried
1 scallion, chopped
1/4 teaspoon salt
1 teaspoon freshly ground black pepper
2 tablespoons balsamic vinegar
2 tablespoons red wine vinegar
1/2 cup extra virgin olive oil
1/4 cup olive oil

In a food processor, add the basil, oregano, scallion, salt, freshly ground black pepper, both vinegars and the extra virgin olive oil. Process until the ingredients are blended and salt is dissolved. Add the olive oil and process again until the mixture slightly thickens. Makes 1 1/3 cups.

Italian Dressing, Raspberry Variation: For special taste treat on green salads, exchange 3 tablespoons of raspberry vinegar for the 2 tablespoons of red wine vinegar.

ROQUEFORT DRESSING

This is good dressing to use on iceberg lettuce salad, since there is no lettuce taste loss. It should be served immediately and not halved.

2 teaspoons cider vinegar
1 cup sour cream
1/4 teaspoon cayenne pepper
1/4 teaspoon salt
freshly ground black pepper to taste
1/2 cup Roquefort cheese, crumbled

Combine the vinegar, sour cream, cayenne pepper, salt and black pepper in a bowl. Stir until the salt dissolves. Add the Roquefort cheese and mix well. Chill for at least 1 hour before serving. Makes 1 1/2 cups.

FOOD PROCESSOR MAYONNAISE

Ordinary homemade mayonnaise is fraught with culinary dangers. The biggest hazard is the mayonnaise can often separate while it is being made or before it is served. Making mayonnaise is a tedious process requiring continuous beating of the oil and vigilance in adding the ingredients. What follows is a simpler and equally tasty alternative.

1 raw egg, both yolk and white
1 teaspoon dry mustard
1/2 teaspoon salt
1/8 teaspoon cayenne pepper
1/2 cup olive oil
2 tablespoons wine vinegar or lemon juice or any combination of the two
2/3 cup extra virgin olive oil

Put the raw egg, mustard, salt and pepper into a food processor. Add half the olive oil and pulse the food processor for three seconds or until all the ingredients are well blended. Slowly add the rest of oil while the processor is running. Add the vinegar and a third of the extra virgin olive oil and pulse again until the mixture has become smooth. Slow add the remaining extra virgin olive oil while processing. Continue processing until the mixture has become thick. Makes 1 1/2 cups.

PINK MAYONNAISE

Pink Mayonnaise adds zest to vegetable, tuna or chicken salads. The recipe may be halved and will store up to three days in the refrigerator.

1 cup mayonnaise
1/4 cup tomato paste
3 tablespoons pimento, minced
1/2 teaspoon fresh lemon juice
1/2 teaspoon Worcestershire sauce
1 clove garlic, minced

Combine the mayonnaise and tomato paste in bowl. Stir until the mixture is well blended. Add the pimento, lemon juice, Worcestershire sauce and garlic. Blend well and serve. Makes 1 1/2 cups.

GREEN MAYONNAISE

Fish and raw vegetable salads are well suited to Green Mayonnaise. Do not halve the recipe.

3 tablespoons fresh spinach, chopped
3 tablespoons fresh watercress, chopped
3 tablespoons scallion, chopped
3 tablespoons parsley, chopped
1 cup mayonnaise
1/8 nutmeg, grated
salt to taste

Put the spinach, watercress, scallion and parsley in a small saucepan. Add just enough water to cover. Quickly bring to a boil and remove from heat. Let stand for one minute. Drain the greens well and put them into a food processor. Process until the greens are pureed. Add the mayonnaise, nutmeg and salt. Pulse until well mixed. Makes 1 2/3 cups.

REAL RUSSIAN DRESSING

Years of bottled Russian dressing have convinced most Americans that is made from ketchup, mayonnaise and chopped pickles. The following recipe is the real thing. It is equally at home with lettuce salads as well as turkey and roast beef sandwiches. This dressing can be refrigerated in a tightly sealed jar for four days.

1 cup mayonnaise
1 tablespoon tomato paste
1 tablespoon red wine vinegar
2 tablespoons Tabasco sauce
1 tablespoon celery, chopped
1 tablespoon onion, minced
3 tablespoons caviar or lumpfish roe
1 tablespoon sour cream
1 teaspoon Worcestershire sauce
1/4 teaspoon salt

Put all the ingredients in a bowl and mix well with a wooden spoon. A food processor or blender will do just as well. Makes 1 1/2 cups.

Real Russian Dressing, Dill Variation: If this is not Russian enough , add 2 tablespoons fresh chopped dill to this recipe.

THOUSAND ISLAND DRESSING

This Thousand Island Dressing is much more flavorful and rich than the bottled version. Those who are used to the commercial variety are in for a tasty surprise. Serve this dressing with any lettuce salad

1 cup mayonnaise
1/4 cup Tabasco sauce
2 tablespoons pimento stuffed green olives, minced
1 hard cooked egg chopped
1 tablespoon heavy cream
1 1/2 tablespoons scallion, minced
2 tablespoons green pepper, finely chopped
2 tablespoons parsley, minced
1/4 teaspoon paprika
1/4 teaspoon freshly ground black pepper

Put the mayonnaise and Tabasco sauce in a medium sized bowl. Stir with a wooden spoon until well blended. Add the olives, egg, cream, and lemon juice. Continue stirring. Add the remaining ingredients and stir until well combined. Refrigerate for at least one hour before serving. Makes 1 1/2 cups.

JUICERS AND SALAD DRESSINGS

A new appliance is making its debut in the kitchen. It is called the juicer. Mostly the juicer is used for making vitamin-and mineral-loaded health drinks. But it is also a valuable aid to fine cuisine. The extracted juices add a lift to all courses from soup to dessert. This of course includes salads and salad dressings. Here are a few dressings made from juices extracted by this latest culinary marvel.

APPLE-BASIL DRESSING

1/2 cup olive oil
1/4 cup apple juice
1 tablespoon fresh basil leaves, chopped
1 tablespoon lemon juice
1/4 teaspoon freshly ground black pepper
1 clove chopped garlic (optional)

Combine all ingredients in a screw-cap jar and shake vigorously until well blended. Let sit for at least one hour to give flavors time to meld and develop. Shake again before dressing salad. Makes 1 cup.

ORANGE-CURRY DRESSING

1/2 cup olive or safflower oil
1/4 cup orange juice
1 teaspoon (or more to taste) curry powder
freshly ground black pepper
1 teaspoon onion juice

Combine all ingredients in a screw-cap jar and shake vigorously until well blended. Let sit for at least one hour to give flavors time to meld and develop. Shake again before dressing salad. Makes 3/4 cup.

Fresh vegetable and fruit juices
add a special zest to salad dressings.

SALAD NOTES

GREEN & VEGETABLE SALADS

Almost any vegetable can be used in a salad. The only require-
ments are that they be fresh. Try to find local produce whenever
possible. Always buy vegetables in season which will be more
flavorful and nutricious than those shipped long distances and
held in cold storage. Lettuces, in particular, should never be
refrigerated if bought fresh. They will last longer and be more
flavorful if kept in a cool, dark place until ready for use.

BEAN SALADS

Beans are one of the oldest known sources of nutrition. They are
high in protein and complex carbohydrates and low in calories
and fat. Equally important, they are delicious to eat in many
different guises. They add an earthy tang to vegetable, fish and
meat salads.

SEAFOOD SALADS

Fish consumption is rising fast as we become more and more
health conscious and aware of the high-quality protein and low fat
in fish foods. When buying fish, always look for the freshest you
can find. The eyes should be bright, smell fresh and scales smooth
and clean.

Shellfish are susceptible to contamination and spoilage and
should be bought from a reputable market. Shellfish such as
shrimp, crabs and lobsters are invariably overcooked. They should
be plunged into boiling water, the heat lowered, and then sim-
mered until done (when the shells have changed color). They will
continue to cook after you remove them from the pot, so be
careful.

Molluscs—clams, oysters, mussels—should cook only until
their shells open. Any that fail to open should be discarded.

PASTA SALADS

Pasta salads have taken the country by storm. It has become
difficult to eat out at lunchtime without finding a few pasta salads
on a menu. Any shape or size of pasta can be used, though
imported Italian pasta cooks up with more "bite" and flavor than
most domestic varieties (after all, they've had longer to practice).
Pasta should be cooked only until *al dente*, literally "to the tooth"
and drained immediately. Coat the pasta with your dressing while
it is still hot. One of the nicest things about pasta is the large
number of combinations of fish, meat, poultry and vegetables
that work with it. You can eat it day after day and never get tired
of the endless combinations.

GRAIN SALADS

Grains—rice, wheat, bburghul, barley, etc.—all make interesting
salad bases. They should be cooked (except burghul) as carefully
as any other food and be kept firm. Dress them while still warm.

MEAT SALADS

Beef, lamb, veal and pork can be used—either as leftovers or freshly cooked—in a wide variety of salads. Pork, especially as it is now bred, is low in fat, lean and tender, and can make a very fine-textured substitute for chicken and other poultry. All meats used in salad will need to be dressed separately first, as otherwise they will tend to be dry, as all leftovers lose moisture when refrigerated. Also, let any leftovers come to room temperature before using, for greater concentration of flavor.

POULTRY SALADS

Chicken, duck, goose, squab, game hens, turkey all make delicious and elegant salads. Freshly cooked, they will be more flavorful and juicy, but leftovers, especially marinated, can be almost equally good. Discard skin and fat for fewer calories and lower cholesterol.

FRUIT SALADS

Seasonal fruits make delicious desserts, either combined with other fruits, juices, liquers, nuts, syrups, etc. or alone, sliced on a bed of greens. Local fruit is always best, and try to get it dead ripe. Fruits picked unripe and shipped long distances never develop the juiciness or savor of the real thing.

CAESAR SALAD

Not a salad in the tradition of Julius, Rome 48 BC, but in the tradition of Caesar Cardini, Tiajuana, circa 1920. Cardini was a restaurateur whose clients were the early legends of Hollywood. This salad is best when done in the theatrical tradition in which it was invented. You make it in front of your guests.

2 large heads of romaine lettuce
1 garlic clove, minced
1/2 cup olive oil, extra virgin olive oil preferred
1/2 teaspoon freshly ground black pepper
1/2 teaspoon salt
2 tablespoons fresh lemon juice
1/2 cup freshly grated Parmesan cheese
6 to 8 anchovy fillets
1/4 teaspoon Worcestershire sauce
2 eggs, raw or hard-cooked, chopped
1 1/2 cups garlic croutons

Pull the lettuce leaves from the stalks and tear them into bite-sized pieces. Put the garlic and oil in jar with a tight fitting lid. Cover and shake well. Set the jar aside. Put the lettuce in a large salad bowl and the rest of the ingredients into individual bowls.

In front of your guests, grind the pepper over the lettuce leaves with a pepper mill. Pour the oil on the lettuce leaves and gently toss, enough to coat each leaf. Sprinkle the lettuce with salt. Add the lemon, Parmesan cheese, anchovy fillets and Worcestershire sauce. Gently toss the salad twice. If you are using raw eggs break them into the salad. If the eggs are hard-cooked add them in a dramatic fashion. Add the croutons, toss and serve. Serves 6-8.

PINE NUTS &
WATERCRESS

Once the pine nuts in this recipe are toasted they can be stored in a small plastic bag and frozen for later use.

1/4 cup pine nuts (pignoli)
2 large bunches watercress
3/4 cup fresh parsley, chopped
1/2 cup fresh chives, minced
3/4 cup Lemon Dressing

Preheat the oven 350°F. Put the pine nuts on a baking sheet and toast them in the oven for 8-10 minutes or until brown. Combine the watercress, parsley and chives in a salad bowl. Add the Lemon Dressing and toss. Add the pine nuts and toss again. Serves 4.

ORANGE & GREENS
SALAD

Refreshing in sight and taste, this salad is an excellent accompaniment to roast lamb or pork. This salad goes well with dry white wine.

1/4 head red leaf lettuce
1/4 head Boston lettuce
2 navel oranges
1 cup carrots cut into strips
1/4 cup sultanas or currants
3/4 cup Paprika Dressing

Tear lettuce into bite-sized pieces. Arrange them in a salad bowl. Peel the oranges and divide them into segments. Cut each segment into halves or thirds. Add the orange pieces, carrots and sultanas to the salad bowl. Toss. Add the Paprika Dressing and toss again. Serves 4.

GARDEN MIXED GREEN SALAD

Almost any fresh salad green may be substituted for those called for in this recipe. It is a substantial salad that can be served alone as light summertime lunch or with veal and beef roast dinners.

1 head Boston or garden lettuce
1 head romaine lettuce
3 Belgian endives
1/4 cup celery, chopped
3 hard-cooked eggs, sliced
1/2 cup watercress, chopped and stems removed
1/2 medium onion, sliced into rings
2 large tomatoes, peeled and cut into wedges
1/2 cup pickled beets, cut into strips
2 tablespoons fresh parsley, chopped
1 1/3 cups Modern Vinaigrette

Line a salad bowl with some lettuce leaves. Tear the remaining lettuce leaves into bite-sized pieces. Add them to the salad bowl. Cut the endives into bite-sized pieces and add to the salad bowl. Add the celery, eggs watercress, onion rings and tomatoes to the salad bowl. Toss gently, pour the Modern Vinaigrette on the salad and toss again. Add the beets and parsley just before you serve. Serves 6-8.

STRING BEAN SALAD

Not only is this a salad, it can also be used as a vegetable entree.

1 pound string beans
3 large tomatoes, peeled, seeded and diced
1 large onion, chopped fine
1/2 cup olive oil
3 tablespoons balsamic vinegar
2 tablespoons fresh chervil,
2 tablespoons fresh tarragon

Cook string beans in plenty of salted water until just tender and drain. Combine while still warm with remaining ingredients and toss well. Let sit, turning occasionally for at least an hour before serving at room temperature. Serves 6.

Top: Endive Salad
Bottom: Mixed Greens & Mushroom Salad

MIXED GREENS
& MUSHROOMS

The Italian Dressing, Raspberry Variation, and roasted pine nuts make this salad extra special

1/2 cup pine nuts (pignoli)
2 heads of Boston lettuce
2 Belgian endives
1 small head radicchio
1/2 cup steamed small mushrooms, sliced
1/3 cup Italian Dressing, Raspberry Variation

Preheat the oven 350°F. Put the pine nuts on a baking sheet and toast them in the oven for 8-10 minutes or until brown. Tear the lettuce and radicchio into bite-sized pieces. Cut the endive into thin slices. Put the greens into a large salad bowl. Add the pine nuts and mushrooms. Pour the dressing over the greens and toss well. Serves 4.

ENDIVE SALAD

A perfect salad before the main course. Endive Salad calls for prosciutto, a type of Italian ham. Prosciutto is noted for its nutty flavor that is both salty and peppery—and unique.

6 heads endive
2 hard-cooked eggs
2/3 cup Apple-Basil Dressing
1/4 pound prosciutto, thinly sliced and diced
1/8 teaspoon salt
1/4 teaspoon freshly ground black pepper
2 tablespoons fresh parsley, chopped

Cut the endives diagonally into 3/4-inch rounds. Arrange the endives on a serving platter. Put the chopped eggs in a bowl and add the dressing. Toss gently. Add the remaining ingredients and heap in the center of the endive rounds. Serves 6.

FENNEL SALAD

The anise-tasting leaves of the fennel plant lend an interesting tang to a salad, especially when teamed with a Pernod vinaigrette.

1 medium fennel
4 radishes, thinly sliced
2 oranges, peeled and sectioned
4 black olives, pitted and halved
3 tablespoons onion, minced
several torn feathers from the fennel stalk
6 tablespoons olive oil
3 tablespoons cider vinegar
1 teaspoon Pernod or anisette
1/4 teaspoon salt
1/8 teaspoon cayenne pepper

Slice the bulb and stalks of the fennel into rings. Place in a serving bowl Arrange the radishes, orange sections, olives, onion, and torn fennel feathers around the sliced fennel rings. In a mixing bowl. Whisk together the oil, vinegar. Pernod, salt and pepper. Pour over the salad and serve. Serves 4.

SNOW PEA SALAD

The bright green snow pea pods in this salad make a colorful accompaniment to fish and chicken dishes. Bamboo shoots, water chestnuts, Chinese cabbage, and snow peas are all staple Asian foods and should be available at better supermarkets.

24 snow peas, fresh or frozen
6-8 marinated artichoke hearts, drained and chopped
1/2 cup bamboo shoots, drained
12 water chestnuts, sliced
3/4 cup Chinese cabbage, shredded
8 large mushrooms, thinly sliced
1 cup Chinese Dressing
4-6 parsley sprigs

In a pan of lightly salted boiling water, cook the snow peas fro one minute or until they turn bright green. Drain well. Rinse the snow peas in very cold water and drain again. Put the snow peas, artichoke hearts, bamboo shoots, water chestnuts, Chinese cabbage and mushrooms in a bowl. Toss. Add the Chinese Dressing and toss again. Garnish with parsley and serve. Serves 6.

COBB SALAD

This is a version of the popular salad served at the Brown Derby restaurant in Hollywood during the 1930s and 1940s. It was invented by the noted American humorist, writer and actor Irving Cobb. There are many variations on the original recipe, but they all have one thing in common: the ingredients are all cut into tiny pieces.

1/2 head iceberg lettuce, torn in pieces
1 head Belgian endive
1/3 head romaine lettuce, torn into bite-sized pieces
2/3 bunch chicory, torn in pieces
2/3 bunch watercress, torn into sprigs
2 medium-sized tomatoes, peeled and diced
3 cups poached chicken breasts, diced
1 green pepper, seeded and finely chopped
1 sweet red pepper, seeded and finely chopped
1/4 cup crisply cooked bacon, crumbled
1/4 cup scallions, minced
1 1/3 cups Modern Vinaigrette

On a large serving platter, arrange the iceberg lettuce, chicory, endive, romaine lettuce and watercress. Add the remaining ingredients, except for the dressing, in either lines, layers or piles. The choice is up to you. Chill for 30 minutes. Add the dressing just before serving. Do not toss. Serves 6-8.

ASIAN SALAD, PEANUT DRESSING

Peanut dressings are very popular in Indonesia. This salad is a distant variation of the Indonesian favorite *Gado Gado*. Although it requires some cooking it is served at room temperature, usually during the hot months of summer.

2 cups romaine lettuce, shredded
1 cup spinach, shredded
4 cups bean sprouts
2 cups green beans, cut into 1—inch pieces
1 cup carrots, sliced into strips
1 cup cucumber, sliced
5 tablespoons peanut oil, vegetable oil may be substituted
1/2 cup onion, minced
1 cup water
3 tablespoons red wine vinegar
1 1/2 teaspoons sugar
3 tablespoons peanuts, ground
1/2 cup peanut butter
1 teaspoon chili powder
1/4 teaspoon salt

Drop the vegetables and lettuce in boiling water. As soon as the water returns to a boil, but no more than ninety seconds later, remove the vegetables and immediately run under very cold water. Drain and place in a salad bowl. In a small skillet sauté the onion in oil until soft. Add the water, vinegar, sugar and ground peanuts. Stir for a few seconds. Stir in the peanut butter, chili powder and salt. Continue stirring until the dressing is well combined. This may take between four or five minutes. Lower the heat and simmer for another minute. Remove and let cool. Pour the dressing on the salad and serve. Serves 4-6.

CALIFORNIA SALAD

This salad is very popular in the Golden State where tomatoes and oranges grow all year round. It is a good accompaniment to meat entrees.

1 pound spinach, leaves torn into bite-sized pieces and stems removed
1/2 head chicory, torn into bite-sized pieces
1 head Boston lettuce, torn into bite-sized pieces
1/2 head romaine lettuce, torn into bite-sized pieces
2 tomatoes, seeded and diced
1 1/2 cups mandarin oranges slices
2 large mushrooms, sliced
2 tablespoons capers, drained
2 tablespoons honey
1 1/3 cups Paprika Dressing

Put all the lettuces in a salad bowl and chill for one hour. Just before serving, remove the salad from the refrigerator and add the tomatoes, oranges, mushrooms and capers. Toss lightly. In a jar with tight fitting lid add the Paprika Dressing and honey. Shake until the honey has combined with the dressing. Pour the dressing on the salad. Serves 8.

SPINACH & BACON SALAD

This is a substantial salad that can be served with a main course or by itself. Served with some chilled white wine, it makes an elegant lunch. This recipe calls for onion juice. To make this, scrape the surface of an onion with the back of knife. The juice will collect on both the knife and on the surface of the onion.

1 pound fresh spinach, leaves torn into bite-sized pieces and stems removed
2 heads red leaf lettuce, leaves torn into bite-sized pieces
1/2 pound crisp-cooked bacon, crumbled
1/4 cup sugar
1 teaspoon salt
1 teaspoon dry mustard
1 tablespoon onion juice
1/3 cup cider vinegar
1 tablespoon poppy seeds
1 cup olive oil

Put the spinach and lettuce in a large salad bowl and add the crumbled bacon. In a large jar with tight fitting lid put the sugar, salt, mustard, onion juice, vinegar, poppy seeds and oil. Shake until the salt and sugar dissolve. Pour the mixture on the salad and toss lightly. Serves 8.

JAPANESE CUCUMBER SALAD

This Asian salad goes well a light late dinner. Some Japanese prefer a very tart taste in this salad. They substitute 3 tablespoons distilled white vinegar instead of 1/4 cup rice wine vinegar.

2 medium-sized cucumbers, thinly sliced
1 1/2 teaspoons salt
1/4 cup rice wine vinegar
2 tablespoons soy sauce
1 teaspoon sugar
2 teaspoons white sesame seeds

Put the cucumber slices in a colander and sprinkle with the salt. Let the cucumbers drain for 30 minutes. Remove the cucumbers and pat dry between two layers of paper towels. In a large jar with tight fitting lid put the vinegar, soy sauce and sugar. Shake until the sugar dissolves. Put the cucumber slices in a bowl and add the dressing. Toss lightly. Toast the sesame seeds in a dry skillet over a high heat. Shake the pan frequently while toasting. When the seeds begin to jump remove the from the pan. Crush them in a pestle or lightly grind them in coffee grinder. Sprinkle the crushed sesame seeds on the salad. Serves 4.

Top: Tomato & Mozzarella Salad
Bottom: Cachcombar

CACHCOMBAR

Serve this Indian tomato and onion salad for a refreshing end to a rich meal. The salad contains onions, lots of them. Garish each plate with a few sprigs of fresh parsley. Parsley is a very effective natural breath freshener.

1 teaspoon fresh ginger, minced
1 tablespoon fresh coriander or parsley, chopped
1/4 cup lime juice
1/4 teaspoon salt
1/4 teaspoon freshly ground black pepper
3 large tomatoes, seeded and sliced
2 medium-sized white onions, sliced into rings
1/4 cup green peppers, chopped
2 hot green chili peppers, seeded and coarsely chopped

Put the ginger, coriander, lime juice, salt and pepper in a jar with a tightly fitting lid. Cover and shake until the salt dissolves. Arrange the tomatoes and onions in rows on a serving dish. Sprinkle with both types of peppers. Pour the lime juice dressing over the salad and let stand for 30 minutes before serving. Serves 4.

TOMATO & ONION SALAD

If you are using vine-ripened, garden-fresh tomatoes, no vinegar is needed for this wonderful first course salad. The natural acidity of the tomatoes will do nicely.

2 to 3 large tomatoes, thinly sliced, the fresher the better
1 large Spanish onion, thinly sliced
3 tablespoons fresh basil, chopped
1/3 cup extra virgin olive oil
4 tablespoons balsamic vinegar, to be used if the tomatoes are not the freshest
1/4 teaspoon salt
1/2 teaspoon freshly ground black pepper

Arrange the tomatoes and onions in alternating layers on a serving dish. Sprinkle the salad with the oil, basil, salt, pepper and vinegar if needed. Serves 4

MOROCCAN PEPPER SALAD

A favorite among Moroccans, this salad goes well with meat stews and couscous.

6 large sweet green peppers
6 large tomatoes
2 medium-sized onions
1/3 cup olive oil
3 tablespoons fresh lemon juice
1 tablespoon ground cumin
1/4 teaspoon hot red pepper flakes, crushed
3/4 teaspoon fresh coriander, chopped
6 black olives
6 anchovy fillets

Preheat the broiler. Put the peppers and tomatoes on a baking sheet and cook, turning the peppers and tomatoes occasionally, until the skins begin to blister. Remove the vegetables from the broiler and set aside to cool. Remove the skins and seeds from the peppers and tomatoes. Chop the tomatoes, peppers and onions. Combine them in a salad bowl. In a large jar with tight fitting lid put the olive oil, lemon juice, cumin, red pepper flakes and coriander. Shake well. Pour the dressing over the salad and toss. Marinate in the refrigerator for one and half hours, tossing occasionally. Remove the salad from the refrigerator and garnish with olives and anchovies. Serves 6-8.

GERMAN
POTATO SALAD

An American potato salad that still bears the name of its country of origin. Serve it with chicken, beef or ham.

4 scallions, minced
1 garlic clove, minced
1 teaspoon capers, drained
2 tablespoons fresh dill, chopped
2 tablespoons fresh parsley, chopped
1 teaspoon salt
1 teaspoon freshly ground black pepper
5 tablespoons vegetable oil
3 tablespoons white wine vinegar
1 tablespoon beef stock
1/2 teaspoon sugar

Cook the potatoes with their skins in a large pot of light salted boiling water. Drain well and either peel and dice the potatoes, or leave the small potatoes whole and unpeeled. Put the potatoes in salad bowl and add the green onions, garlic, capers, dill, and parsley. Toss lightly. In a large jar with tight fitting lid put the salt, pepper, oil, vinegar, beef stock and sugar. Shake until the sugar and salt dissolve. Pour the dressing over the salad and toss. Let stand at room temperature for one and half hours before serving. Serves 6.

MIDDLE EASTERN COLESLAW

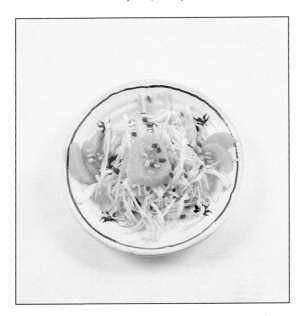

This Middle Eastern version of coleslaw is a far cry from the usual bland stuff served with a watery mayonnaise dressing. It keeps its freshness on even the hottest days. Serve this cole-slaw with meat main courses, especially those that are barbecued or broiled.

3 cups cabbage, coarsely shredded
2-3 tablespoons salt
1 cup fresh orange juice
3 tablespoons lemon juice
1/4 teaspoon sugar
1/2 teaspoon honey
1 teaspoon hot red pepper flakes
1 tablespoon white wine vinegar
1/2 teaspoon salt

Put the shredded cabbage in a colander. Sprinkle the 2-3 table-spoons of salt over the cabbage. Toss and let stand for one hour. Rinse the salt from the cabbage. Drain. Wrap the cabbage in kitchen towel and squeeze as much liquid from the cabbage as possible. Put the remaining ingredients in a salad bowl. Stir until the sugar and honey dissolve. Add the cabbage and toss. Serves 4-6.

HAM & VEGETABLE PASTA SALAD

A good way to use leftover ham and an excellent summer-time main course. Serve this salad with a German Mosel or Rhine white wine.

1 pound pasta shapes, cooked
2 tablespoons extra virgin olive oil
1 cup uncooked peas
1 cup raw carrots, sliced
1 cup broccoli florets
1 cup cooked ham, cubed
1/4 cup grated Parmesan cheese
2 tablespoons fresh parsley, chopped
1 1/4 cup Italian Dressing
1 teaspoon freshly ground black pepper

Put the cooked pasta in a salad bowl and add the olive oil. Toss to coat the pasta well. Cook the pea, carrots and broccoli in a large pan of boiling water until just tender, about eight to ten minutes. Drain and rinse with cold water. Drain again. Add the vegetables, ham, cheese and parsley to the pasta. Toss until well mixed. Add the Italian Dressing and lightly toss. Serves 6.

CRAB MEAT SALAD, CAPER DRESSING

The caper dressing in this salad will work equally well over cooked lobster meat. Serve the salad with a dry white wine for brunch or as a first course at dinner.

5 cups romaine lettuce, torn into bite-sized pieces
11/2 cup cooked crab meat, still warm
1/2 cup olive oil
3 tablespoons red wine vinegar
3 tablespoons drained capers
1 garlic clove, finely chopped
1/4 teaspoon salt
1/2 teaspoon dried oregano
freshly ground black pepper to taste

Put the romaine lettuce and the crab meat in salad bowl. Loosely mix and set aside. In a saucepan combine the olive oil, vinegar, capers, garlic, salt, oregano, and pepper. Heat just to the boiling point and quickly remove the saucepan from the flame. Pour the warm dressing over the lettuce and crab meat. Toss well and serve at once. Serves 4.

TABOULEH

Tabouleh is a Lebanese dish served at picnics throughout the Middle East. It is made from burghul wheat, nuggets of whole wheat that have been steamed and broken up. If the wheat had been ground instead it would have become whole wheat flour. Fresh mint is crucial to this salad. It can be increased to taste, but never decreased.

1 cup burghul wheat
2 cups boiling water
1/2 cup scallions, chopped
5 tablespoons fresh mint, chopped
2 medium-sized tomatoes, seeded and chopped
1 cup fresh parsley, chopped
5 tablespoons extra virgin olive oil
6 tablespoons fresh lemon juice
1/2 teaspoon salt
1/2 teaspoon freshly ground black pepper
10 large lettuce leaves
10 black olives

Put the burghul in a bowl and add the boiling water. Stir, cover the bowl and let stand for 35 minutes. Drain the wheat, squeezing out any remaining water between your palms. Put the burghul in a bowl. Add the scallions, mint, tomatoes and parsley. Toss gently. Serves 4-6.

SPANISH CHICKEN SALAD

Leftover chicken returns to table as an entree salad. It is a complete meal made from a very flexible recipe.

3 cups cooked chicken, shredded
1/2 cup salami, cubed
3 medium-sized boiled potatoes, peeled and diced
1 green pepper, seeded and coarsely chopped
1/2 cup pimento, chopped
1 cup cooked green peas
2 radishes, thinly sliced
2 tablespoons capers, drained
1/2 cup pimento-stuffed green olives, quartered
3 tablespoons dry sherry
1/2 cup olive oil, extra virgin olive oil preferred
1/4 cup white wine vinegar
1/4 teaspoon ground white pepper
1 large head Boston lettuce
2 hard-cooked eggs, chopped
6-8 cooked asparagus spears
8 fresh parsley sprigs
1 medium-sized onion, sliced into rings

Put the chicken, salami, potato, chopped pepper, pimento, green peas, radishes, capers and olives in a mixing bowl. Toss once. Put the sherry, olive oil, vinegar and white pepper in a jar with a tightly fitting lid. Cover and shake until well mixed. Pour the dressing over the salad and toss again. Cover and chill for four hours. Line a serving platter with lettuce leaves. Add the chopped eggs to the salad in the mixing bowl and toss lightly. Drain any excess dressing from the bottom of the mixing bowl and transfer the salad to the serving plate. Garnish with the asparagus spears, parsley sprigs and onion rings. Serves 6-8.

CELERY & RADISH SALAD

This crisp and refreshing salad is perfect as an accompaniment to roast or grilled meats or chicken.

2 cups celery, sliced thin
1 bunch radishes, sliced thin
1 clove garlic, finely chopped
1 teaspoon sharp mustard
1/2 cup olive oil
2 tablespoons wine vinegar
freshly ground black pepper to taste

In a bowl, combine the celery and radishes. In a small jar, combine the remaining ingredients; cover and shake well. Pour the dressing over the vegetables and toss well. Let sit at least 1/2 hour for the flavors to mingle. Serves 4.

Top: *Curried Apricot & Chicken Salad*
Bottom: *Oriental Pork Salad*

CURRIED APRICOT & CHICKEN SALAD

A chilled white wine is a good accompaniment to this main-course salad. If your tastes run to spicier foods, add 1 tablespoon of ground cardamom and 1/8 teaspoon of cayenne pepper in with the curry powder.

4 chicken breasts, skinned and boned
4 tablespoons sweet butter
1 cup unflavored yogurt
1/4 cup curry powder
1 teaspoon salt
1/4 teaspoon freshly ground black pepper
1/2 pound seedless green grapes
2 cups dried apricots, cut in strips
2 cups mandarin orange segments
1 cup cashews
1 cup apricot liqueur
6-8 lettuce leaves

Cut the chicken breasts into 1-inch cubes. Melt the butter in a large skillet. Add the chicken and cook over a moderate to low heat, turning often, until the cubes are firm, but not brown. This may take seven to ten minutes. Transfer the chicken to a large mixing bowl, using a slotted spoon. Combine the yogurt and curry powder in a separate small bowl. Add the yogurt and curry to the chicken in the mixing bowl. Season with salt and pepper, and more curry, if desired. Add the remaining ingredients , except the lettuce, to the chicken. Toss until all the are components well coated. Cover and refrigerate for at least one hour. Line a serving dish with the lettuce leaves and serve. Serves 4-6.

ORIENTAL PORK SALAD

The Chinese never eat uncooked greens, but the flavors of this salad are unmistakably Chinese.

2 cups bean sprouts
1 carrot, shredded
2 cups roast pork, shredded
2 tablespoons peanut butter
3 tablespoons warm water
1/2 teaspoon salt
1 tablespoon sugar
1 teaspoon honey
1 tablespoon sesame seed oil
1 1/2 tablespoons white wine vinegar
1 tablespoon peanut oil
1 teaspoon Tabasco sauce
2 cloves garlic, finely chopped
3 tablespoons chopped green onion

Blanch the bean sprouts and carrots in boiling water, drain and dry. Line a serving platter with the bean sprouts and carrots. Mound the roast pork on top. Combine all the remaining ingredients in a screw top jar and shake vigorously until well-blended. Pour over the vegetables and pork and serve. Serves 4-6.

MUSSEL SALAD

Mussels are one of the best sources of low-fat protein around. They are also very cheap. This makes a main course salad perfect for a summer's eve.

6 pounds mussels
1 cup white wine
2 cloves garlic, peeled
1 large onion, finely chopped
1 red pepper, peeled, seeded and cut in strips
1 cup olive oil
1/4 cup wine vinegar
1/2 teaspoon freshly ground black pepper
1 tablespoon capers, drained and rinsed

Scrub the mussels well, removing the beards. Place them in a large pot with the white wine, garlic, onion and red pepper. Bring to a boil, pot covered, and cook until the mussels open, a matter of only a few minutes. When cool enough to handle, remove the mussels from their shells, discarding any that haven't opened or have broken shells, and place in a large bowl. Strain the broth and add the remaining vegetables to the mussels. Add the oil, vinegar, pepper and capers and toss well. Let cool to room temperature before serving. If you must refrigerate this salad, let it stand for an hour out of the refrigerator before serving for the flavors to develop. Serves 4.

CALAMARI SALAD

Calamari, or squid, is one of the most plentiful and cheapest of all seafood. To often, it is prepared carelessly, resulting in rings of rubbery flesh. Carefully cooked and imaginatively dressed, calamari are a delicious change of pace.

2 pounds baby squid, cleaned, ink sac removed and cut into rings
1 quart water
1 bay leaf
1 clove garlic, peeled and crushed
1 half lemon
1 cup olive oil
3 tablespoons lemon juice
1/2 teaspoon freshly ground pepper
2 ounces sun dried tomatoes in oil, cut into strips

In a large pot combine the squid, water, bay leaf, garlic and lemon. Bring to a boil, then reduce heat and simmer gently for 10 minutes. Drain and discard everything but the squid. Combine the squid in a bowl with the oil, lemon juice, pepper and sun dried tomatoes and toss well. Let stand for an hour and serve. Serves 4.

TUNA SALAD

The old standby, tuna salad, can be made remarkably different if you use the best tuna, homemade mayonnaise and interesting seasonings.

2 7-ounce cans tuna in olive oil
1/4 cup celery, finely chopped
1 medium sweet onion, finely chopped
1/2 cup mayonnaise
freshly ground black pepper to taste

Drain the tuna and flake into a mixing bowl. Add the remaining ingredients and mix well. Can be served as a main course salad or as a filling for sandwiches. Serves 2 as a salad, or fills 4 sandwiches generously.

SALAME SALAD

All the preserved pork products of the world, whether the rarefied silkiness of genuine Parma ham or simple summer sausage, make excellent appetizer salads. With a touch of potato salad and some good, crusty bread they are fit for a delicious light lunch.

1/4 pound Genoa salame, thinly sliced
2 eggs, hard boiled and halved
lettuce leaves
1 carrot, peeled and shredded

On a shallow or flat plate, arrange the salame in rolls. Arrange the other ingredients around the salame. This can be varied with other salads or garnishes and can be served plain or dressed with oil and vinegar. Serves 1.

SPROUT & WALNUT SALAD

The crunchiness of sprouts—bean, alfalfa or pea—coupled with the richness of walnut meats makes an unusual and luxurious salad.

6 cups sprouts
3/4 cup walnut meats, roughly chopped
1 recipe Modern Vinaigrette

Place sprouts and walnuts in a salad bowl. Add dressing and toss lightly. Serves 4.

CLAM & PASTA SALAD

Although it looks like a plate of hot pasta with white clam sauce, this salad is really an easy to make, cool refreshing summer variation. Shrimp and/or mussels may be substituted or added according taste.

1/2 pound pasta shapes, cooked and drained
1/2 cup extra virgin olive oil
1/2 pound cooked clams, chopped
3 tablespoons fresh lemon juice
1 1/2 garlic cloves, minced
3 tablespoons fresh parsley, chopped
2 tablespoons fresh basil, chopped
1 tablespoon fresh mint, chopped
3 tablespoons freshly grated Parmesan cheese
1/2 teaspoon salt
1 teaspoon freshly ground black pepper

Put the pasta in a large salad bowl and add one tablespoon of the olive oil. Lightly toss, add the clams and toss again. Put the remaining olive oil, lemon juice and garlic in a jar with a tightly fitting lid. Cover and shake until well mixed. Add the parsley, basil, mint, Parmesan cheese salt and pepper. Shake again until blended. Pour the dressing over the salad and toss again. Serve at once or, chill up to two hours before serving. Serves 4-6.

LINGUINI SALAD

This makes a perfect impromptu luncheon salad for those unexpected summertime guests.

4 large tomatoes, seeded and coarsely chopped
1/4 cup marinated artichoke hearts, drained and chopped
4 teaspoons parsley, chopped
1 cup Italian Dressing
1 teaspoon Tabasco sauce
1 pound linguini (thin noodles)

Put the tomatoes, artichoke hearts and parsley in a salad bowl. Add the Tabasco sauce to the Italian Dressing and pour over the tomatoes and artichoke hearts. Let stand at room temperature for one hour. Cook the linguini in large pot of boiling water until just tender. Drain well and add the linguini to the salad bowl. Toss well and serve. Serves 4-6

ITALIAN
RICE SALAD

In Italy, this salad would be made with *arborio*, a short grain rice.
If you cannot find a suitable short grain rice, long grain or even
brown rice will work just as well.

1 1/2 cups cooked rice
1/2 cup cooked ham, cubed
1 tablespoon drained capers
1 large tomato, seeded and chopped
1/4 cup freshly grated Parmesan cheese
3 tablespoons olive oil
3 tablespoons fresh lemon juice
1/2 teaspoon salt
1/2 teaspoon black pepper
1 tablespoon fresh parsley, chopped
1/2 cup marinated artichoke hearts, drained and chopped

Put the rice, ham, capers, tomatoes, and Parmesan cheese in a
salad bowl. Toss lightly. Put the olive oil, lemon juice, salt, pepper
and parsley in a jar with a tightly fitting lid. Cover and shake until
well mixed. Pour the dressing over the salad and let stand for one
hour. Serves 6.

Top: Italian Fontina Salad
Bottom: Lentil & Feta Salad

ITALIAN FONTINA SALAD

Fontina is a mild, velvet-textured cheese produced in northern Italy. It combines well with other ingredients in a solid or melted state. Serve this salad with a light dry red wine.

2 large yellow peppers, seeded and halved
2 large red peppers, seeded and halved
1/2 pound Fontina cheese, diced
1/4 cup pitted green olives, thinly sliced
1/3 cup olive oil, extra virgin preferred
1 1/2 teaspoons Dijon-style mustard
3 tablespoons cream
1 tablespoon scallion, chopped
3/4 teaspoon salt
1 teaspoon freshly ground black pepper
1 tablespoon fresh parsley, chopped

Preheat the broiler. Place the peppers on a baking sheet and broil for 10 to 15 minutes or until the skins are blistered and slightly blackened. Remove the peppers from the heat. When the peppers are cool enough to handle, removed the blistered skin. Cut the peppers into thin strips and place in a serving bowl. Add the Fontina cheese and olives. Toss once. In a large jar with tight fitting lid put the olive oil, mustard, cream, scallion, salt and black pepper. Shake until salt dissolves. Pour the dressing over the salad and toss. Chill the salad for one hour. Garnish with chopped parsley and serves. Serves 6

LENTIL &
FETA SALAD

Feta is a common cheese in the Middle East and Greece. It is readily available from cheese shops and better markets.

1 1/2 cups brown lentils
1 bay leaf
1/2 teaspoon dried basil
2 garlic cloves, crushed
1/2 cup celery, diced
1 small onion, chopped
1/2 cup fresh chives, chopped
3/4 cup feta cheese, crumbled
6 tablespoons extra virgin olive oil
3 tablespoons red wine vinegar
1/8 teaspoon oregano
1/2 teaspoon salt
1/2 teaspoon freshly ground black pepper

Put the lentils in a bowl and add two and half cups of water. Soak the lentils for two hours. Drain. In saucepan, put the soaked lentils and enough cold water to cover. Add the bay leaf, basil, and one garlic clove. Bring to a boil and simmer, covered, for 20 minutes. Add the celery and onion. Again, pour just enough water on the lentil mixture to cover. Cover the saucepan and cook for 10 more minutes. Drain and discard the bay leaf and garlic clove. Serves 4.

GERMAN
BEEF SALAD

This substantial main course salad can be served with a small green salad.

2 tablespoons Dijon style mustard
1/2 cup beef stock
5 tablespoons vegetable oil
1/4 cup red wine vinegar
1/2 teaspoon salt
1/2 teaspoon freshly ground black pepper
2 pounds cooked beef, cubed
2 large tomatoes, diced
2 hard-cooked eggs, chopped
2 large boiled potatoes, peeled and diced
2 small onions, minced
10 small sweet gherkins, minced
1/2 cup fresh parsley, chopped

In a large jar with tight fitting lid put the mustard, vegetable oil, vinegar, salt and pepper. Shake until the salt dissolves. Put the beef, tomatoes, eggs, potatoes, onions and gherkins in a salad bowl and toss. Pour the dressing over the salad. Toss again. Cover the bowl and chill for one and half hours. Toss lightly and garnish with parsley. Serves 6

EGG SALAD

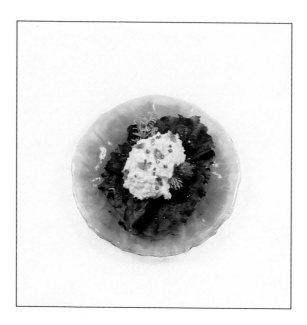

Anchovies are a sprightly touch, adding tang and saltiness to a creamy, bland mixture.

6 hard-boiled eggs, chopped
1/2 cup celery, chopped
3 anchovy fillets, chopped
3 tablespoons green onion, chopped
1/2 cup mayonnaise
1/8 teaspoon cayenne pepper
1/2 teaspoon freshly ground black pepper

Put the egg, celery, anchovies and green onion in a mixing bowl and toss gently. Add the remaining ingredients and toss until well mixed. Chill for 1 hour. Serves 4.

WALDORF SALAD

This enduring classic was first served at the famed Waldorf Astoria Hotel in New York as an appetizer. It's also good as an accompaniment to ham and pork.

3 tart apples, cored and diced (do not peel)
2 cups celery, chopped
1/2 cup walnuts, coarsely chopped
3 tablespoons raisins
3 tablespoons lemon juice
3/4 cup mayonnaise
1 teaspoon salt
1/2 teaspoon freshly ground black pepper

Place all in the ingredients in a mixing bowl and toss until well coated. Chill for 1 hour. Serve on lettuce leaves on individual plates. Serves 4-6.

SALADE NICOISE

This salad has as many variants as there are cooks. Traditionally served as a lunch salad in the South of France, it has been modified over the years into all sorts of atrocities. Here's the real thing.

7 ounce can tuna fish in oil, drained
6 anchovy filets
2 hard-boiled eggs
2 tomatoes, cut into wedges
1/2 pound string beans, blanched
4 artichoke hearts
1/2 pound boiled new potatoes, quartered
1/4 pound mushrooms, sliced
1/2 recipe Classic French Vinaigrette
oil-cured black olives for garnish

Arrange the ingredients in separate heaps on a flat platter. Pour over the vinaigrette. Garnish with olives. Serves 2.

CHICK PEA SALAD

Chick peas add a nutty, satisfying quality to many dishes. Here, they are used in salad in the style of Provence, with North African overtones.

1/4 cup raisins
2 1/2 cups cooked chick peas
1/2 cup sweet red pepper, diced
1/2 cup green onions, finely chopped
2 tablespoons pimento, chopped
3 tablespoons parsley, chopped
1/3 cup olive oil
3 tablespoons lemon juice
1/2 teaspoon dried thyme
1/2 teaspoon freshly ground black pepper

Soak the raisins in a small bowl in cold water to cover for 30 minutes, drain well. Combine the chick peas, red pepper, raisins, green onion, pimento and parsley in a salad bowl and toss. Put the olive oil, lemon juice, thyme and pepper in a jar with a tight-fitting lid. Cover and shake well until blended. Pour over the salad and toss well to coat. Chill for 1 hour. Serves 6.

ICEBERG LETTUCE & RUSSIAN DRESSING

The classic diner salad cannot be ignored. There are times when this is exactly what one needs to bring back memories of blue plate specials and shiny chrome counters.

1 head iceberg lettuce
1 recipe Russian Dressing

Discard the outer leaves of the lettuce. Cut the head into quarters. Place each quarter on a separate salad plate (ice cold, of course) and douse with Russian Dressing.

Top: Melon Salad, Ginger Sauce
Bottom: Pear Salad

MELON SALAD, GINGER SAUCE

An excellent way to finish a poultry dinner.

3/4 cup whipping cream
1 teaspoon fresh lemon juice
1 tablespoon superfine sugar
1/8 teaspoon cayenne pepper
3 large pieces preserved ginger, chopped
1/2 cup almonds, chopped
1 large honeydew melon, peeled, seeded and cubed

Put the cream, lemon juice, sugar, and cayenne pepper in a mixing bowl. Whisk or beat the cream until it becomes thick but not stiff. Add the ginger and the almonds, reserving one tablespoon of the almonds. Continue to whisk or beat until the cream becomes stiff. Cover the bowl and chill until ready to serve. Arrange the melon on a serving dish and chill for 30 minutes. Just before serving, top the melon cubes with the ginger cream. Sprinkle the reserved almonds on top and serve. Serves 6-8.

PEAR SALAD

An unusual juxtaposition of fruit and vegetables, this light and refreshing salad is an ideal starter.

4 Barlett pears
1 clove garlic, crushed
1 teaspoon salt
1 1/2 teaspoons sugar
1/2 teaspoon dried tarragon, crumbled
1/2 teaspoon dried basil, crumbled
1/4 cup red wine vinegar
1/4 cup olive oil
1/4 cup water
2 tablespoons sherry
1 cup celery, chopped
1 cup green pepper, chopped
1/2 cup scallions, chopped
2 large ripe tomatoes, finely chopped
4 romaine lettuce leaves, chilled

Wash the pears and refrigerate. Combine the garlic, salt, and sugar in a mixing bowl. Add the tarragon, basil, vinegar, oil, water and sherry. Whisk until well blended. Transfer the liquid to a jar and let stand for one hour. Put the celery, green pepper, scallions and tomatoes in a bowl and chill for one hour. Remove the vegetables from the refrigerator and pour the dressing on top of them. Toss. Place one lettuce leaf on each of four serving plates. Halve and core the pears. Arrange two pear halves, cut side up, on each lettuce leaf. Top with the dressed vegetables. Spoon the remaining dressing over the pears and serve. Serves 4.

Top: Champagne & Peach Salad
Bottom: Sunshine Fruit Salad

CHAMPAGNE & PEACH SALAD

Although this recipe calls for champagne, you don't have to use your best. Also, you may substitute three cups of sliced strawberries, when in season, for the six peaches. As a dessert this salad is wonderful with a small cup of rich espresso coffee.

6 ripe peaches, peeled, pitted and thinly sliced
3 tablespoons fresh orange juice
1 tablespoon fresh lime juice
1/8 teaspoon cinnamon
1 tablespoon superfine sugar
2 cups Champagne

Prick the peach slices with a fork and set aside. In a jar with a tight fitting lid, put the orange juice, lime juice, cinnamon and sugar. Cover and shake until all the ingredients are well mixed. Put the peaches in a serving bowl and add the orange juice mixture. Pour the Champagne on the peaches and toss gently. Cover the bowl and chill the salad for two to three hours. Serve in small bowls. Serves 6

SUNSHINE FRUIT SALAD

A multihued golden sunset in a small dessert salad.

2 grapefruits
1 cup bananas, thinly sliced
1/2 cup mandarin orange segments
1 cup pineapple wedges
1 tablespoon cherries finely chopped
3 tablespoons pure maple syrup
1 tablespoon créme de cacao
4 red cherries

Halve the grapefruits. Carefully remove the segments without piercing the skin. Separate the white membrane from the segments and discard. Seed and break apart the segments. Reserve the grapefruit skin-shells. Combine the grapefruit, banana, mandarin orange, pineapple and chopped cherries in a mixing bowl. Toss lightly. Add the maple syrup and créme de cacao. Toss lightly again. Fill the grapefruit shells with the fruit salad. Top each salad with a whole cherry. Refrigerate until ready to serve. Serves 4.

THE AUTHOR

Lionel Martinez is a New York writer and photographer. Among his many books are *Easy & Elegant Entertaining, Sensational Salads* and *The Complete Juicer*.